Node.js BACKEND DEVELOPMENT

A Complete Step-by-Step Guide for Beginners

CHAPTER 1

INTRODUCTION TO BACKEND DEVELOPMENT AND NODE.JS

... ensure that it sets a solid foundation, without overwhelming beginners

1.1   Understanding   Backend Development

In this section, we'll introduce the concept of backend development and the essential role it plays in web applications. This foundational knowledge will help you understand how Node.js fits into the bigger picture.

What is Backend Development?

Definition: Backend development involves creating the server-side of an application. This is where data is processed, stored, and served to the user-facing (frontend) side of the application.

Key Responsibilities: Backend developers handle tasks like data storage, server logic, authentication, and communication with the frontend.

Core Components of a Backend System

Servers: The machine (or service) that hosts the backend and responds to user requests.

Databases: Where information is stored for easy access and retrieval.

APIs: Methods of communication between different parts of an application, allowing the frontend to access backend data and functions.

Backend Technologies Overview

Brief overview of backend programming languages (JavaScript, Python, Java, etc.) and technologies (Node.js, Django, etc.), with a focus on Node.js.

Explain the key reasons why JavaScript and Node.js have become popular for backend development.

Exercise: Think of a web application you frequently use (like an online store). What might its backend need to do? Write down a few tasks (e.g., handling payments, storing user profiles).

1.2 What is Node.js?

Definition and Key Features of Node.js

Definition: Node.js is an open-source, cross-platform runtime environment for executing JavaScript on the server-side.

Asynchronous, Non-blocking: Node.js uses an asynchronous, non-blocking event model, allowing it to handle multiple tasks simultaneously without waiting for one to finish.

Why Use Node.js for Backend Development?

Single Programming Language (JavaScript): Allows developers to use JavaScript for both frontend and backend.

Fast and Scalable: Due to its non-blocking I/O operations, Node.js is efficient and can handle many simultaneous connections.

Vibrant Ecosystem: npm, Node.js's package manager, offers thousands of libraries and modules that make development faster and easier.

Note: Real-World Applications of Node.js

Discuss a few real-world use cases (e.g., streaming services, social media applications, real-time chats) where Node.js is commonly used.

> **Exercise:** Write a short paragraph on why you think using the same language (JavaScript) for frontend and backend might be beneficial.

1.3 Setting Up Your Environment

Before you can start building with Node.js, you'll need to install both Node.js and npm

(Node Package Manager). The following guide walks you through each step for Windows, macOS, and Linux.

Step-by-Step Guide: Installing Node.js and npm

Installing Node.js and npm on Windows

1. Download Node.js:

Open your browser and go to the official Node.js website.

You'll see two versions available for download:

LTS (Long-Term Support): This version is stable and recommended for most users.

Current: This version has the latest features but may be less stable.

Click on the LTS version to start downloading the installer (usually named node-vxx.x.x-x64.msi).

2. Run the Installer:

Once the download is complete, open the .msi file.

Follow the setup wizard:

Accept the License Agreement.

Choose an installation location (the default is fine for most users).

Check the box to add Node.js to your PATH. This will allow you to use Node.js commands from any folder in your system.

3. Verify the Installation:

Open Command Prompt or PowerShell.

Type the following commands and press Enter:

    node -v

This command should display the installed Node.js version, e.g., v18.17.1.

    npm -v

This command should display the installed npm version, e.g., 9.6.7.

If both versions display, Node.js and npm are successfully installed!

Installing Node.js and npm on macOS

1. Download Node.js:

Go to the Node.js website.

Download the LTS version for macOS.

2. Run the Installer:

Open the downloaded .pkg file.

Go through the installer steps:

Agree to the license.

Select the installation location (default is fine).

Finish the installation by following the prompts.

3. Verify the Installation:

Open Terminal.

Run the following commands:

    node -v

This will display the Node.js version, confirming it's installed.

    npm -v

This will display the npm version, indicating npm is also installed.

"Alternative Option: If you're comfortable using package managers, you can install Node.js using Homebrew. Run the command brew install node in the terminal. This method will install both Node.js and npm".

Installing Node.js and npm on Linux

1. Using the NodeSource Repository (Recommended for Debian/Ubuntu):

Open Terminal and add the NodeSource repository for the latest LTS version:

curl   -fsSL
https://deb.nodesource.com/setup_lts.x | sudo
-E bash -

Install Node.js and npm with:

sudo apt install -y node.js

2. Verify the Installation:

Run the following commands to check the installation:

    node -v

This shows the installed Node.js version.

    npm -v

This shows the installed npm version.

"Alternative Installation Method for Other Distributions: Visit Node.js download page for specific instructions for your Linux distribution. Most distributions support Node.js installation via their package managers or Node Version Manager (NVM)".

Understanding npm (Node Package Manager)

After installation, you have both Node.js and npm on your system. Here's a quick overview of npm:

npm is a package manager included with Node.js, allowing you to download libraries (called "packages") that can extend the functionality of your application.

You can install packages either globally (for all projects on your system) or locally (just for a specific project).

Testing npm by Installing a Package:

1. Open your terminal or command prompt.

2. Type the following command to install a popular package, nodemon:

```
npm install -g nodemon
```

The -g flag installs it globally, making nodemon available across all projects.

3. Verify installation by running:

```
nodemon -v
```

If you see a version number, nodemon was installed successfully!

What is nodemon?: nodemon is a useful tool for development that automatically restarts your Node.js application whenever you make changes to your code. This saves you the time of stopping and restarting the server manually.

With Node.js and npm now installed, you're ready to begin exploring Node.js in the upcoming sections.

This step-by-step guide ensures that even a beginner can set up Node.js and npm confidently, regardless of their operating system. Let me know if you'd like additional clarifications or setup details!

> **Exercise:** Practice installing a simple package globally by running npm install -g nodemon and explain what nodemon does (it helps restart the server automatically when files change).

1.4 Your First Node.js Program

Creating a "Hello World" Application

Step-by-Step Guide:

Open a new directory for your project.

Create a new file called app.js.

Write the following code in app.js:

```
console.log("Hello, World!");
```

Running Your Program:

Open a terminal, navigate to your project directory, and run:

```
node app.js
```

Explain what's happening: Node.js is executing the app.js script and logging the message to the console.

Experimenting with Console Output

Variables in Node.js:

Introduce the let and const keywords, and demonstrate how to declare and print variables.

```
const name = "Node.js Beginner";
```

console.log("Hello, " + name + "!");

Basic Debugging with Console.log():

Encourage beginners to use console.log() to see how their code is behaving.

> **Exercise:** Try creating a few variables and log them to the console. Change the values and re-run the code to see how it changes output.

1.5 Understanding JavaScript Basics (for Backend)

Since Node.js is JavaScript-based, a solid understanding of JavaScript basics is essential for backend work. This section covers key JavaScript concepts with hands-on examples.

JavaScript Essentials

Data Types and Variables:

Introduce common data types (string, number, boolean, array, object) and variable declarations using let and const.

Example:

```
let age = 25;

const name = "Node.js";

console.log(name + " is " + age + " years old.");

Control Structures:

If-else statements:

const isAdmin = true;

if (isAdmin) {

  console.log("Access granted");

} else {
```

```
console.log("Access denied");
```

```
}
```

Loops (e.g., for, while): Demonstrate loops with simple examples to manipulate data, like printing numbers 1-10.

Functions and Modules

Creating Functions:

Explain how to define and use functions to modularize code.

```
function greet(name) {

  return "Hello, " + name;

}
```

```
console.log(greet("Node.js Beginner"));
```

Introduction to Modules:

Show how to create reusable modules by exporting functions.

Example:

```
// greeting.js

module.exports = function (name) {

  return "Hello, " + name;

};

// app.js

const greet = require("./greeting");

console.log(greet("Node.js Beginner"));
```

Asynchronous JavaScript Basics

Callbacks and Promises:

Briefly explain asynchronous behavior, callbacks, and introduce Promise syntax in a simple example.

Example:

```
const fetchData = () => {

  return new Promise((resolve) => {

    setTimeout(() => {

      resolve("Data fetched!");

    }, 2000);

  });

};

fetchData().then((data) => console.log(data));
```

> Exercise: Create a function that simulates fetching data using a Promise and setTimeout. Test it to understand how asynchronous code works.

Summary

In this chapter, you have:

Learned what backend development is and why Node.js is popular for it.

Installed Node.js and npm on your computer.

Written your first Node.js program and learned how to run it.

Explored JavaScript basics relevant to Node.js, such as data types, control structures, functions, and asynchronous programming.

End-of-Chapter Challenge: Try modifying your "Hello World" program to take a name as input and greet that name. Practice using variables, functions, and console.log() to make it interactive.

CHAPTER 2

JAVASCRIPT FUNDAMENTALS FOR NODE.JS

... designed to introduce the essential JavaScript fundamentals for backend development with Node.js. This chapter builds on the setup from Chapter 1, ensuring beginners have a solid understanding of JavaScript basics before diving into Node.js-specific features.

2.1 Why JavaScript is Essential for Node.js

Node.js uses JavaScript as its core programming language. Understanding JavaScript is crucial because:

Consistency: You can use JavaScript for both frontend and backend, which streamlines development.

Flexibility: JavaScript supports asynchronous programming, making it ideal for handling multiple tasks simultaneously in Node.js.

Efficiency: JavaScript's non-blocking I/O model allows Node.js to perform high-speed operations.

2.2 Setting Up Your First JavaScript Program

Before jumping into JavaScript concepts, let's practice by writing and running some simple JavaScript code.

1. Create a New File:

Inside your Node.js project directory, create a new file called basics.js.

2. Write a Basic Script:

In basics.js, add the following code:

console.log("Welcome to JavaScript with Node.js!");

3. Run the Script:

Open a terminal, navigate to your project folder, and type:

node basics.js

You should see the message "Welcome to JavaScript with Node.js!" printed in the terminal.

> **Exercise:** Try editing the message in basics.js and re-run the code to see the changes in the terminal.

2.3 JavaScript Variables and Data Types

Declaring Variables:

JavaScript variables can be created using let, const, or var. For modern JavaScript (ES6+), we primarily use let and const.

let: Used for variables that can be reassigned.

const: Used for constants that cannot be reassigned after initial assignment.

Example:

let age = 25;

const name = "Node.js";

console.log(name + " is " + age + " years old.");

Basic Data Types in JavaScript:

1. **String:** Text data (e.g., "Hello, World!")

2. **Number:** Numeric data, including integers and decimals (e.g., 42, 3.14)

3. **Boolean:** True or false values (true, false)

4. **Array:** A collection of values (e.g., [1, 2, 3, 4])

5. **Object:** Key-value pairs for structured data (e.g., { name: "Node.js", age: 12 })

> **Exercise:** Create a variable of each type in basics.js and use console.log() to print each one. Experiment with reassigning let variables.

2.4 Control Structures in JavaScript

Control structures allow you to define how your program should behave based on certain conditions.

If-Else Statements:

If-else statements let you execute code based on conditions.

Example:

let isAdmin = true;

if (isAdmin) {

  console.log("Access granted.");

} else {

  console.log("Access denied.");

}

Switch Statements:

Switch statements are useful for handling multiple conditions in a cleaner way.

Example:

```
let day = "Monday";

switch (day) {

  case "Monday":

    console.log("It's the start of the week!");

    break;

  case "Friday":

    console.log("Weekend is coming soon.");

    break;

  default:

    console.log("Have a great day!");

}
```

Loops: for and while:

Loops allow you to repeat a block of code multiple times.

For loop: Repeats code a specific number of times.

```
for (let i = 0; i < 5; i++) {

  console.log("Iteration number: " + i);

}
```

While loop: Repeats code as long as a condition is true.

```
let count = 0;

while (count < 3) {

  console.log("Count is: " + count);

  count++;

}
```

Exercise: Create a small program that prints numbers from 1 to 10 using a loop.

2.5 Functions and Scope

Functions allow you to group code into reusable blocks, which can be called with specific values (arguments) and return results.

Defining Functions: To create a function in JavaScript

Function Declaration:

```
function greet(name) {

  return "Hello, " + name + "!";

}

console.log(greet("Student"));

Arrow Function (ES6+):


const greet = (name) => {

  return "Hello, " + name + "!";

};
```

```
console.log(greet("Student"));
```

Understanding Scope:

Variables defined inside a function are local to that function, while those outside are global.

Example:

```
const globalVar = "I am global";

function showScope() {

  const localVar = "I am local";

  console.log(globalVar); // Accessible

  console.log(localVar);  // Accessible

}

showScope();

console.log(globalVar);   // Accessible

console.log(localVar);       // Error: localVar is
not defined
```

> **Exercise**: Create a function that takes two numbers as arguments and returns their sum. Test it by logging the result.

2.6 Introduction to Asynchronous JavaScript

In Node.js, asynchronous programming is essential. It allows your application to handle multiple tasks at once, like processing user requests while performing database operations.

Callback Functions

A callback is a function passed into another function to be executed later.

Example:

```
function fetchData(callback) {

  setTimeout(() => {
```

```
callback("Data received!");

}, 2000);

}

fetchData((message) => {

    console.log(message); // Runs after 2 seconds

});
```

Promises

Promises represent a value that may be available in the future. They simplify asynchronous code and make it easier to handle success and error cases.

Example:

```
const fetchData = () => {

    return new Promise((resolve, reject) => {

        setTimeout(() => {

            resolve("Data fetched successfully!");
```

```
  }, 2000);

 });

};
```

```
fetchData()

  .then((message) => console.log(message))

  .catch((error) => console.log(error));
```

> **Exercise**: Create a function that returns a Promise, simulating a delay before resolving with a success message.

Summary

In this chapter, you've learned the following JavaScript fundamentals:

Variables and data types: How to store and manage different types of data.

Control structures: Using if-else, switch, and loops to direct the flow of your code.

Functions and scope: Creating reusable blocks of code and understanding variable scope.

Asynchronous programming: Using callbacks and promises to handle tasks that take time to complete.

These fundamentals will help you write more effective and organized JavaScript code, which is essential as you move forward into more complex Node.js applications.

End-of-Chapter Challenge: Create a mini-project in basics.js that combines everything you've learned:

Define an array of names.

Use a loop to print a greeting for each name.

Create a function that simulates fetching data for each name with a delay (use setTimeout or a Promise).

CHAPTER 3

INTRODUCTION TO NODEJS CORE CONCEPTS

... aimed at introducing Node.js core concepts and running the first server. This chapter builds directly on the JavaScript fundamentals from Chapter 2 and serves as the gateway to understanding the Node.js runtime.

3.1 Understanding the Node.js Runtime Environment

Node.js is a powerful runtime that allows JavaScript to run outside of a web browser, typically on servers. Let's break down why it's useful for backend development.

Why Node.js?

Non-blocking I/O: Node.js uses an asynchronous, non-blocking I/O model, allowing it to handle multiple requests efficiently.

JavaScript Everywhere: With Node.js, you can use JavaScript for both client-side and server-side code.

Community and Libraries: The Node.js ecosystem is extensive, with libraries available for nearly any feature or functionality.

How Node.js Executes JavaScript Code

Node.js uses the V8 JavaScript engine, originally developed for Google Chrome, to execute JavaScript at high speed.

It operates on a single-threaded event loop model, which makes it lightweight and efficient for handling many connections at once.

> **Exercise:** Research more on the advantages and common use cases of Node.js in backend development.

3.2 The Node.js Event Loop and Asynchronous Programming

The event loop is what makes Node.js "non-blocking." Understanding this concept is crucial for writing efficient Node.js code.

What is the Event Loop?

The event loop continuously checks for tasks, executing any ready code and deferring other tasks until they are ready.

This allows for handling multiple operations (like file I/O, database queries) without waiting for each one to finish before starting the next.

Demonstrating the Event Loop in Action

Create a new file named eventLoopDemo.js:

```
console.log("Start");

setTimeout(() => {

  console.log("Inside the setTimeout callback");

}, 2000);

console.log("End");
```

Run the Code: Run eventLoopDemo.js using the terminal:

node eventLoopDemo.js

You'll notice that "End" prints immediately after "Start," even though the setTimeout is delayed. This is due to the asynchronous nature of Node.js.

Exercise: Experiment with different delay times in setTimeout and observe how the code behaves.

3.3 Modules and the CommonJS Module System

Modules are reusable blocks of code. Node.js uses the CommonJS module system to organize and share code between files.

Creating and Exporting Modules

1. Create a file named greetings.js:

```
const sayHello = (name) => {

  return `Hello, ${name}!`;

};

module.exports = sayHello;
```

2. Create another file named app.js:

```
const greet = require('./greetings');

console.log(greet("Student"));
```

3. Run the Program:

```
node app.js
```

You should see the output: Hello, Student!

Using Built-in Node.js Modules

Node.js includes several built-in modules, like fs (file system), http (for creating servers), and path (for handling file paths).

Example using the fs module:

```
const fs = require('fs');

fs.writeFileSync('example.txt',          'Hello,
Node.js!');

console.log("File created successfully.");
```

> **Exercise:** Experiment with creating and reading files using the fs module.

3.4 Building a Simple HTTP Server

Now that we've explored modules, let's build a basic HTTP server in Node.js. This will be your first step into server development.

1. Create a new file: server.js

2. Write the Following Code:

```
const http = require('http');

const server = http.createServer((req, res) => {

  res.writeHead(200, { 'Content-Type': 'text/plain' });

  res.end('Hello, World! Welcome to Node.js Server');

});

server.listen(3000, () => {

  console.log("Server is listening on port 3000");
```

});

3. Run the Server:

node server.js

4. Access the Server:

Open a web browser and go to http://localhost:3000.

You should see the message "Hello, World! Welcome to Node.js Server" without the quotes.

Understanding the Code

http.createServer(): This method creates a new HTTP server.

req and res Parameters: req (request) represents the client's request, while res (response) represents the server's response.

res.writeHead(): Sets the HTTP status and headers.

res.end(): Sends the response body and signals the end of the response.

> **Exercise**: Change the server message to "Hello from your first Node.js server!" and test the output.

3.5 Handling Basic Routing

Routing allows us to define different responses for different URL paths.

1. Modify server.js to Add Routing:

```
const http = require('http');

const server = http.createServer((req, res) => {

  if (req.url === '/') {

    res.writeHead(200,      {      'Content-Type':
'text/plain' });

    res.end('Welcome to the Home Page');
```

```javascript
  } else if (req.url === '/about') {

    res.writeHead(200,    {    'Content-Type':
'text/plain' });

    res.end('Welcome to the About Page');

  } else {

    res.writeHead(404,    {    'Content-Type':
'text/plain' });

    res.end('Page Not Found');

  }

});


server.listen(3000, () => {

  console.log("Server is listening on port
3000");

});
```

2. Test Different Routes:

Go to http://localhost:3000/ to see the home page message.

Go to http://localhost:3000/about for the about page.

Test an undefined route, like http://localhost:3000/unknown, to see the 404 error message.

> **Exercise**: Add another route for /contact that returns "Contact us at contact@example.com."

3.6 Basic Error Handling

Handling errors is critical in server development to avoid crashing the application unexpectedly.

1. Simulate an Error:

Modify your server.js to include a potential error:

```
const http = require('http');

const server = http.createServer((req, res) => {

  try {

    if (req.url === '/error') {

      throw new Error("This is a test error!");

    }

    res.writeHead(200, { 'Content-Type': 'text/plain' });

    res.end('Hello, Node.js!');

  } catch (error) {

    res.writeHead(500, { 'Content-Type': 'text/plain' });

    res.end("Server Error: " + error.message);
```

```
  }

});

server.listen(3000, () => {

  console.log("Server is listening on port
3000");

});
```

2. Test the Error Handling:

Go to http://localhost:3000/error in your browser. You should see the error message displayed instead of crashing the server.

> **Exercise**: Modify the error handling to log the full error details to the console but only display a generic message to the user.

Summary

In this chapter, you've learned the core concepts of Node.js:

The Node.js runtime and its single-threaded, non-blocking I/O model.

The event loop, which handles asynchronous tasks efficiently.

Modules and the CommonJS system, enabling reusable code.

Building a basic HTTP server with Node.js and handling basic routing.

Basic error handling to keep your server running smoothly.

These concepts form the backbone of backend development in Node.js, and with this foundation, you're ready to dive deeper into creating more complex APIs and server applications.

End-of-Chapter Challenge: Expand your server by adding a new route /time that returns the current date and time. Then, add error handling that logs unexpected errors to a file instead of displaying them to the user.

CHAPTER 4

WORKING WITH THE FILE SYSTEM AND CORE MODULES

... introduce file handling and essential modules in Node.js, building on the foundational concepts covered in previous chapters.

4.1 Introduction to the File System Module

Node.js includes a built-in module, fs (file system), that allows you to work with the file system. This includes creating, reading, updating, and deleting files, which is crucial for backend tasks like logging, storing temporary data, and serving files.

Basic File Operations

Creating a File: Use fs.writeFile() or fs.writeFileSync() to create and write data to a new file.

Reading a File: Use fs.readFile() or fs.readFileSync() to read the contents of a file.

Updating a File: You can append or replace content using fs.appendFile() or fs.writeFile() respectively.

Deleting a File: Use fs.unlink() to delete a file.

Example: Creating and Reading a File

1. Create a new file fileSystemDemo.js.

2. Write the following code:

```
const fs = require('fs');
```

// Writing to a file

```
fs.writeFileSync('sample.txt', 'Hello, this is a sample file created with Node.js!');
```

```
console.log('File created successfully.');
```

// Reading the file

```
const data = fs.readFileSync('sample.txt', 'utf8');
```

```
console.log('File Content:', data);
```

3. Run the file in your terminal:

```
node fileSystemDemo.js
```

You should see output confirming the file creation and then displaying its content.

> **Exercise:** Try creating multiple files, then read them all to understand how file handling works in practice.

4.2 Handling Files Asynchronously

Node.js encourages asynchronous operations to avoid blocking the main thread. Using asynchronous file handling functions ensures better performance, especially in web applications with many users.

Using Async Methods for File Operations

Async versions of file handling methods include fs.writeFile(), fs.readFile(), and fs.unlink().

These methods take a callback function to handle the results after the operation completes.

Example: Writing and Reading Files Asynchronously

1. Update fileSystemDemo.js with the following code:

```
const fs = require('fs');

// Asynchronously write to a file

fs.writeFile('sampleAsync.txt', 'Hello from async Node.js!', (err) => {

  if (err) throw err;
```

```
console.log('File written asynchronously.');

// Asynchronously read the file

fs.readFile('sampleAsync.txt', 'utf8', (err, data)
=> {

  if (err) throw err;

  console.log('Async File Content:', data);

});

});
```

2. Run the file:

```
node fileSystemDemo.js
```

Notice how the asynchronous callbacks keep the code non-blocking.

> **Exercise**: Try modifying the code to append content to sampleAsync.txt instead of overwriting it.

4.3 Exploring Other Core Node.js Modules

Beyond file handling, Node.js provides other essential modules that support backend tasks. Let's look at some key modules commonly used in backend development.

The Path Module

The path module helps with working with file paths, which is especially useful for handling cross-platform file structures.

Example of Path Module Usage:

```
const path = require('path');

const filePath = path.join(__dirname,
'sample.txt');
```

console.log('File Path:', filePath);

const ext = path.extname(filePath);

console.log('File Extension:', ext);

path.join() joins different path segments into a single path.

path.extname() retrieves the extension of the file.

> **Exercise**: Experiment with different file paths and retrieve directory names using path.dirname().

The OS Module

The os module provides information about the operating system, such as CPU architecture, memory, and network interfaces.

Example of OS Module Usage:

const os = require('os');

console.log('OS Platform:', os.platform());

console.log('OS Architecture:', os.arch());

console.log('Free Memory:', os.freemem());

console.log('Total Memory:', os.totalmem());

> **Exercise:** Try using the os.cpus()
> method to get information about CPU
> cores.

4.4 Creating a Simple File Logger

Let's put these modules into practice by creating a basic file logger, which will be useful in real-world backend applications to track server events or errors.

Logger Project: Writing Logs to a File

1. Create a new file logger.js.

2. Write the following code:

```
const fs = require('fs');

const path = require('path');

const logFilePath = path.join(__dirname, 'logs.txt');

function logMessage(message) {

  const timeStamp = new Date().toISOString();

  const logEntry = `${timeStamp} - ${message}\n`;

  fs.appendFile(logFilePath, logEntry, (err) => {

    if (err) throw err;

    console.log('Log written:', message);
```

```
});
}
```

```
// Usage Example

logMessage('Server started');

logMessage('New user connected');
```

3. Run the logger:

```
node logger.js
```

Every time you run logger.js, it appends a new entry with a timestamp to logs.txt.

Exercise: Modify the logger to include log levels like "INFO," "WARN," and "ERROR."

4.5 Error Handling in File Operations

Error handling is essential in backend applications to ensure that unexpected issues do not cause the application to crash.

Using Try-Catch for Sync Methods

When working with synchronous methods, use try-catch blocks to handle errors.

Example:

```
const fs = require('fs');

try {

  fs.writeFileSync('/protected/sample.txt',
'Trying to write to a protected area');

} catch (err) {

  console.error('Error:', err.message);

}
```

Handling Errors with Async Callbacks

With asynchronous methods, handle errors in the callback function.

Example:

```
fs.readFile('nonexistent.txt', 'utf8', (err, data) => {

  if (err) {

    console.error('Error reading file:', err.message);

    return;

  }

  console.log('File Content:', data);

});
```

> **Exercise:** Simulate an error by trying to read a non-existent file, and then handle it gracefully using async error handling.

4.6 Project: Building a Simple File-Based Data Storage

Now let's build a small file-based storage system that mimics a mini-database. This will store JSON data in files, simulating basic data persistence.

1. Create a new file dataStorage.js.

2. Add the following code:

```
const fs = require('fs');

const path = require('path');

const dataFilePath = path.join(__dirname, 'data.json');

function saveData(data) {

  const jsonData = JSON.stringify(data, null, 2);

  fs.writeFile(dataFilePath, jsonData, (err) => {
```

```
if (err) throw err;

console.log('Data saved.');

});

}


function readData() {

if (!fs.existsSync(dataFilePath)) return null;

const rawData = fs.readFileSync(dataFilePath, 'utf8');

return JSON.parse(rawData);

}

// Test the storage system

saveData({ name: 'Student', age: 20 });

console.log('Retrieved Data:', readData());
```

3. Run the Program:

node dataStorage.js

4. Verify that data.json is created with the stored data.

> **Exercise**: Extend this system to allow adding multiple entries, and implement a method to delete an entry by key.

Summary

In this chapter, you have learned:

How to work with the Node.js file system module for file creation, reading, updating, and deletion.

The difference between synchronous and asynchronous file handling and the importance of non-blocking code in Node.js.

Core Node.js modules like path and os, which help with file paths and system information.

Practical applications like creating a file logger and building a basic file-based data storage.

This chapter has equipped you with fundamental skills for managing files and data in Node.js, crucial for any backend system.

End-of-Chapter Challenge: Build a mini file-based note-taking app where users can add, retrieve, and delete notes, with all operations logged to a file.

Node.js Backend Development
A Complete Step-by-Step for Beginners

CHAPTER 5

BUILDING HTTP SERVERS WITH NODE.JS

... cover the creation of HTTP servers in Node.js, handling requests and responses, and an introduction to RESTful APIs.

Page 78

5.1 Understanding HTTP and Node.js as a Server

Node.js enables you to create and manage web servers that respond to HTTP requests. Before diving into coding, let's break down some essentials:

HTTP (HyperText Transfer Protocol): HTTP is the protocol used by the web to communicate between clients (like browsers) and servers. It operates using methods like GET, POST, PUT, and DELETE, each intended for specific types of requests.

Node.js as a Server: Node.js's built-in http module allows us to create and manage HTTP servers without needing any external library, making it efficient for backend development.

"**Real-world use:** Almost every web application you encounter — from social media to e-commerce platforms — relies on HTTP servers to deliver data to users and handle their interactions".

5.2 Setting Up Your First HTTP Server

Creating an HTTP server with Node.js is straightforward using the http module. This server will listen for incoming requests and respond with a message.

Example: Basic HTTP Server

1. Create a new file called basicServer.js. Write the following code:

```
const http = require('http');

const server = http.createServer((req, res) => {

  res.statusCode = 200;
```

```javascript
res.setHeader('Content-Type', 'text/plain');

res.end('Hello, World! This is your Node.js server responding.');

});

const PORT = 3000;

server.listen(PORT, () => {

  console.log(`Server running at http://localhost:${PORT}/`);

});
```

1.   Run the server:

```
node basicServer.js
```

2.   Open your browser and go to http://localhost:3000. You should see the message "Hello, World! This is your Node.js server responding."

Explanation:

http.createServer() initializes a server.

res.statusCode sets the response status (200 means "OK").

res.setHeader() defines the content type.

res.end() sends the response and closes the connection.

> **Exercise:** Modify the message to include a personalized greeting or a current timestamp.

5.3 Handling Requests and Responses

When a server receives a request, it can handle different aspects of it, including the URL path and HTTP method. This lets you respond differently depending on the request.

Example: Handling Multiple Routes

1. Update basicServer.js:

```
const http = require('http');

const server = http.createServer((req, res)
=> {

  res.setHeader('Content-Type',
'text/plain');

  if (req.url === '/' && req.method ===
'GET') {

    res.statusCode = 200;

    res.end('Welcome to the Home Page');

  } else if (req.url === '/about' &&
req.method === 'GET') {

    res.statusCode = 200;

    res.end('This is the About Page');

  } else {
```

```
res.statusCode = 404;

res.end('Page Not Found');

}

});

const PORT = 3000;

server.listen(PORT, () => {

console.log(`Server          running          at
http://localhost:${PORT}/`);

});
```

2. Run the server and test different routes:

Go to http://localhost:3000/ to see the home page.

Go to http://localhost:3000/about to see the about page.

Visit a non-existent page like http://localhost:3000/unknown to see the 404 message.

Explanation:

req.url and req.method provide information about the requested path and HTTP method.

This setup allows the server to handle multiple routes with specific responses.

> **Exercise**: Add a new route, /contact, that displays a contact message.

5.4 Working with Query Parameters

Query parameters are key-value pairs appended to the URL, used to send additional data to the server. In Node.js, we can parse these parameters to tailor responses.

Example: Parsing Query Parameters

1. Update basicServer.js to handle a query parameter:

```
const http = require('http');

const url = require('url');

const server = http.createServer((req, res) => {

  const parsedUrl = url.parse(req.url, true);

  const name = parsedUrl.query.name || 'Guest';

  res.setHeader('Content-Type', 'text/plain');

  if (parsedUrl.pathname === '/greet' && req.method === 'GET') {

    res.statusCode = 200;
```

```
    res.end(`Hello, ${name}! Welcome to our
site.`);

  } else {

    res.statusCode = 404;

    res.end('Page Not Found');

  }

});

const PORT = 3000;

server.listen(PORT, () => {

  console.log(`Server        running        at
http://localhost:${PORT}/`);

});
```

2. Run the server and navigate to:

   http://localhost:3000/greet?name=John to
   see a personalized greeting.

http://localhost:3000/greet to see a default greeting if no name is provided.

> **Exercise:** Add a new query parameter (e.g., age) and display it in the greeting message.

5.5 Building a Simple RESTful API

A RESTful API allows applications to communicate over HTTP by using structured endpoints for data retrieval and manipulation. Each HTTP method represents a specific action:

GET: Retrieve data.

POST: Submit new data.

PUT: Update existing data.

DELETE: Delete data.

Example: Creating a Simple In-Memory API

1. Create apiServer.js:

```
const http = require('http');

const url = require('url');

let items = [];

const server = http.createServer((req, res)
=> {

  const parsedUrl = url.parse(req.url, true);

  res.setHeader('Content-Type',
'application/json');

  if (parsedUrl.pathname === '/items' &&
req.method === 'GET') {

    res.statusCode = 200;

    res.end(JSON.stringify(items));
```

```
  } else if (parsedUrl.pathname === '/items'
&& req.method === 'POST') {

  let body = '';

  req.on('data', chunk => {

    body += chunk.toString();

  });

  req.on('end', () => {

    const item = JSON.parse(body);

    items.push(item);

    res.statusCode = 201;

    res.end(JSON.stringify({ message: 'Item
added', item }));

  });

  } else {

  res.statusCode = 404;
```

```
      res.end(JSON.stringify({    error:    'Not
Found' }));

  }

});

const PORT = 3000;

server.listen(PORT, () => {

  console.log(`API    Server    running    at
http://localhost:${PORT}/`);

});
```

2. Test the API:

   GET   Request:
   http://localhost:3000/items to retrieve
   all items (returns an empty array
   initially).

   POST Request: Use a tool like
   Postman or curl to add an item.

curl -X POST http://localhost:3000/items -H "Content-Type: application/json" -d '{"name": "Sample Item", "price": 100}'

After posting, use the GET request again to verify that the item is added.

Explanation:

GET /items: Retrieves all items in the in-memory array.

POST /items: Adds a new item to the array by parsing JSON data from the request body.

> **Exercise**: Add PUT and DELETE methods to modify or remove items based on an ID.

5.6 Error Handling in HTTP Servers

When building robust APIs, it's crucial to handle errors gracefully to avoid exposing internal details or crashing the server.

Implementing Basic Error Handling

Modify apiServer.js:

```
const handleErrors = (res, message,
statusCode = 500) => {

  res.statusCode = statusCode;

  res.end(JSON.stringify({ error: message
}));

};



// Usage example within a POST request

req.on('end', () => {

  try {
```

```
const item = JSON.parse(body);

if (!item.name || !item.price) {

  throw new Error('Invalid data');

}

items.push(item);

res.statusCode = 201;

res.end(JSON.stringify({ message: 'Item
added', item }));

} catch (err) {

handleErrors(res, err.message, 400);

}

});
```

Exercise: Add error handling to check if item details are valid (e.g., name and price fields are not empty).

Summary

In this chapter, you've learned:

The basics of setting up an HTTP server in Node.js and handling requests and responses.

How to parse URLs and query parameters to create dynamic responses.

The essentials of building a simple RESTful API, including methods like GET

CHAPTER 6

INTRODUCTION TO EXPRESS.JS

... Covering Express.js; The popular framework for building efficient and scalable web applications with Node.js

6.1 What is Express.js and Why Use It?

Express.js is a lightweight and flexible Node.js web application framework that simplifies the process of building APIs and web applications. It provides a layer of features that streamline handling HTTP requests and responses, managing routes, and integrating middleware.

Why Use Express.js?

Easy Routing: Express offers a straightforward way to manage routing in your application.

Middleware Support: It supports middleware, which is essential for handling requests, responses, and additional logic.

Scalability: Express is modular and extendable, making it ideal for applications of all sizes.

Large Community: Express has a robust community, making it easy to find resources and plugins.

"Real-world use: Express is widely used in production environments to create everything from RESTful APIs to full-featured web applications".

6.2 Setting up Express.js

To start using Express in your project, you need to install it via npm and set up a basic Express server.

1. Initialize a new Node.js project (if you haven't already done so in the current directory):

    npm init -y

2. Install Express:

    npm install express

3. Create a new file called server.js and write the following code:

```
const express = require('express');

const app = express();

const PORT = 3000;

app.get('/', (req, res) => {

  res.send('Hello, Express.js!');

});

app.listen(PORT, () => {

  console.log(`Server is running on http://localhost:${PORT}`);

});
```

4. Run the server:

```
node server.js
```

5. Test it in your browser by going to http://localhost:3000. You should see "Hello, Express.js!" displayed.

Explanation:

app.get('/', ...): Sets up a GET route for the root URL (/).

app.listen(PORT, ...): Starts the server on the specified port.

> **Exercise:** Modify the message in the response or add a new route to respond with a different message.

6.3 Understanding Routes and HTTP Methods in Express

Express makes it easy to define routes and manage HTTP methods. Routes represent different paths in your application, each performing a specific action.

Example: Setting Up Routes for GET, POST, PUT, and DELETE

1. Update server.js:

```
app.get('/greet', (req, res) => {

  res.send('Hello! Welcome to our API.');

});

app.post('/submit', (req, res) => {

  res.send('Data received successfully.');

});

app.put('/update', (req, res) => {

  res.send('Data updated successfully.');

});

app.delete('/delete', (req, res) => {
```

```
    res.send('Data deleted successfully.');

});
```

2. Test each route:

   Open http://localhost:3000/greet in your browser to see the GET response.

   Use Postman or curl to test POST, PUT, and DELETE routes.

Explanation:

GET: Typically retrieves data.

POST: Used to submit new data.

PUT: Updates existing data.

DELETE: Deletes specified data.

> **Exercise**: Add another route that returns the current date and time when accessed.

6.4 Working with Middleware in Express

Middleware functions in Express are functions that run between the client request and the server response. They are useful for tasks like logging, parsing JSON, authentication, and error handling.

Example: Using Built-in Middleware

Express comes with built-in middleware that you can use right away, such as express.json() for parsing JSON data.

1. Update server.js:

   ```
   const express = require('express');

   const app = express();
   ```

```
const PORT = 3000;

// Enable JSON parsing for incoming requests

app.use(express.json());

app.post('/data', (req, res) => {

  const receivedData = req.body;

  res.send(`Received                    data:
${JSON.stringify(receivedData)}`);

});

app.listen(PORT, () => {

  console.log(`Server is running on
http://localhost:${PORT}`);

});
```

2. Test it by sending a POST request with JSON data:

   curl -X POST http://localhost:3000/data -H "Content-Type: application/json" -d '{"name": "John", "age": 25}'

3. Expected Response:

   Received data: {"name": "John", "age": 25}

Explanation:

app.use(express.json()): Enables JSON parsing, allowing Express to automatically parse incoming JSON data.

> **Exercise:** Add a custom middleware that logs each incoming request's method and path.

6.5 Handling Static Files in Express

In web applications, static files like images, stylesheets, and JavaScript files are often served to clients. Express provides an easy way to serve these files from a designated folder.

Example: Serving Static Files

1. Create a directory called public and add an index.html file inside it with some basic HTML content.

2. Update server.js to serve static files:

```
const express = require('express');

const app = express();

const PORT = 3000;



// Serve files from the 'public' directory

app.use(express.static('public'));
```

```
app.listen(PORT, () => {

  console.log(`Server is running on
  http://localhost:${PORT}`);

});
```

3. Run the server and access http://localhost:3000/index.html to see your HTML file.

Explanation:

app.use(express.static('public')): Tells Express to serve any files in the public directory directly to the client.

> **Exercise:** Add a CSS file to public and link it in your index.html.

6.6 Setting Up a Basic REST API with Express

With Express, you can easily create a RESTful API to manage data. Let's create a simple in-memory API to manage a list of users.

Example: Basic REST API

1. Update server.js:

```
const express = require('express');

const app = express();

const PORT = 3000;

app.use(express.json());


// Sample data

let users = [];

// GET all users

app.get('/users', (req, res) => {
```

```
  res.json(users);

});

// POST a new user

app.post('/users', (req, res) => {

  const user = req.body;

  users.push(user);

  res.status(201).json({    message:    'User
added', user });

});

// PUT (update) a user by ID

app.put('/users/:id', (req, res) => {

  const userId = parseInt(req.params.id);

  const updatedUser = req.body;

  users = users.map(user => (user.id ===
userId ? updatedUser : user));
```

```
    res.json({ message: 'User updated',
updatedUser });

});

// DELETE a user by ID

app.delete('/users/:id', (req, res) => {

  const userId = parseInt(req.params.id);

  users = users.filter(user => user.id !==
userId);

  res.json({ message: 'User deleted' });

});

app.listen(PORT, () => {

  console.log(`Server is running on
http://localhost:${PORT}`);

});
```

2. Test each endpoint:

   GET /users: Retrieves all users.

POST /users: Adds a new user (use JSON data with fields like id, name, etc.).

PUT /users/:id: Updates an existing user by id.

DELETE /users/:id: Deletes a user by id.

Explanation:

GET: Lists all users.

POST: Adds a new user.

PUT: Updates an existing user.

DELETE: Removes a user.

> **Exercise:** Add error handling to ensure each request includes valid data before modifying the users array.

Summary

In this chapter, we covered:

Setting up Express.js and building a basic server.

Creating routes and using different HTTP methods.

Working with middleware to handle JSON data and serve static files.

Building a simple RESTful API with Express, including GET, POST, PUT, and DELETE methods

With Express, you're now able to create more complex and scalable applications quickly. You're ready to handle user interactions, data management, and static content, laying a solid foundation for any backend application.

CHAPTER 7

WORKING WITH DATABASES (MONGODB & MONGOOSE BASICS)

... focuses on databases, specifically MongoDB, and using Mongoose as an Object Data
Modelling (ODM) library to interact with MongoDB.

7.1 Introduction to Databases and MongoDB

In backend development, data persistence is crucial. Databases store information that can be retrieved and manipulated, making your applications dynamic. For this book, we'll be using MongoDB, a popular NoSQL database known for its flexibility and scalability.

Why MongoDB?

Document-Oriented: MongoDB stores data as JSON-like documents, making it ideal for working with JavaScript-based applications.

Schema-less: This flexibility allows you to store data without needing a fixed schema.

Scalable and Fast: MongoDB is designed for high performance, making it a popular choice for web applications.

"Real-world use: MongoDB is used by companies like Uber, LinkedIn, and eBay for fast data handling and scalability".

7.2 Setting Up MongoDB

Installing MongoDB Locally

1. **Download MongoDB:** Go to MongoDB's official website and download the MongoDB Community Server suitable for your operating system.
2. **Install MongoDB:** Follow the installation instructions for your operating system.
3. Start MongoDB:

"For macOS and Linux, you may start MongoDB using the command: Mongod"

For Windows, you can run MongoDB as a service or start it from the Command Prompt.

Using MongoDB Atlas (Cloud Option)

MongoDB Atlas is a cloud version of MongoDB. It's convenient and free for small projects.

1. **Create an Account on MongoDB Atlas:** Go to MongoDB Atlas and create a free account.
2. **Create a Cluster:** Select the free cluster option.
   Choose your cloud provider and region.
   Name your cluster and create it.
3. **Connect to the Cluster:** After the cluster is created, choose "Connect" and follow the instructions to get your connection string.

Keep the connection string handy, as you'll need it to connect from your Node.js app.

> **Exercise:** Try setting up a MongoDB Atlas cluster and connect to it via MongoDB Compass, a GUI for managing MongoDB databases.

7.3 Introduction to Mongoose and Why It's Useful

Mongoose is an ODM library for MongoDB, allowing you to define schemas and models in Node.js. It provides a structured way to work with MongoDB data and simplifies CRUD operations.

Why Use Mongoose?

Schemas: Mongoose helps define data structures (schemas) for MongoDB, enforcing some level of consistency.

Built-in Validation: Allows you to validate data before saving it.

Query Building: Simplifies complex queries with its powerful API.

7.4 Setting Up Mongoose in a Node.js Project

1. Install Mongoose:

   npm install mongoose

2. Connecting to MongoDB:

   Create a new file called database.js or add the following to your main server file.

Replace <Your_Connection_String> with your MongoDB connection string (from MongoDB Atlas or local MongoDB).

const mongoose = require('mongoose');

mongoose.connect('<Your_Connection_String>', {

  useNewUrlParser: true,

  useUnifiedTopology: true

})

```
.then(() => console.log('MongoDB connected'))

.catch(err    =>    console.error('MongoDB
connection error:', err));
```

3. Running the Connection Code:

   Run node server.js or your main file to
   ensure the connection to MongoDB is
   successful.

Tip: To make your application modular, keep
the connection code in a separate file and
import it where needed.

7.5 Creating a Simple Mongoose Model

In Mongoose, a Model represents a MongoDB
collection, and a Schema defines the structure

of documents within that collection. Here's how to create a simple user model.

1. Define a User Model: Create a file named models/User.js.

```
const mongoose = require('mongoose');

const userSchema = new mongoose.Schema({

  name: {

    type: String,

    required: true

  },

  email: {

    type: String,

    required: true,

    unique: true

  },
```

```
  age: {

    type: Number,

    required: false

  }

});

const  User  =  mongoose.model('User',
userSchema);

module.exports = User;
```

Explanation:

Name: Required field of type String.

Email: Required field of type String, with the unique property to prevent duplicates.

Age: Optional field of type Number.

> **Exercise:** Try adding additional fields (e.g., password or createdAt) to understand schema creation.

7.6 CRUD Operations with Mongoose

With the model set up, let's perform basic CRUD operations: Create, Read, Update, and Delete.

Creating a New User (Create)

1. Add a Route in your server file:

```
const express = require('express');

const mongoose = require('mongoose');

const User = require('./models/User');

const app = express();

app.use(express.json());

app.post('/users', async (req, res) => {
```

```
try {

  const user = new User(req.body);

  await user.save();

  res.status(201).json(user);

  } catch (error) {

  res.status(400).json({          error:
error.message });

  }

});
```

2. Explanation:

new User(req.body): Creates a new instance of the User model with data from the request body.

await user.save(): Saves the new user to MongoDB.

Reading Users (Read)

Add a GET Route to retrieve all users:

```
app.get('/users', async (req, res) => {

  try {

    const users = await User.find();

    res.json(users);

  } catch (error) {

    res.status(500).json({              error:
error.message });

  }

});
```

Explanation:

User.find(): Retrieves all documents from
the users collection.

Updating a User (Update)

1. Add a PUT Route to update a user by ID:

```
app.put('/users/:id', async (req, res) => {

  try {

    const user = await User.findByIdAndUpdate(req.params.id, req.body, { new: true });

    res.json(user);

  } catch (error) {

    res.status(400).json({ error: error.message });

  }

});
```

2. Explanation:

findByIdAndUpdate: Finds a user by their ID and updates it with the provided data.

The { new: true } option returns the updated document.

Deleting a User (Delete)

1. Add a DELETE Route to delete a user by ID:

```
app.delete('/users/:id', async (req, res) => {

  try {

    await User.findByIdAndDelete(req.params.id);

    res.json({ message: 'User deleted' });

  } catch (error) {

    res.status(500).json({                    error:
error.message });
```

```
    }

  });
```

Explanation:

findByIdAndDelete: Finds a user by ID and deletes them from the collection.

> **Exercise:** Experiment with error handling by trying to retrieve or update users with invalid IDs.

7.7 Validating and Structuring Data with Mongoose

Mongoose provides built-in validation, ensuring that data adheres to the schema before being saved.

Example: Adding Validation to the User Schema

Update the userSchema with validation rules:

```
const userSchema = new mongoose.Schema({

  name: {

    type: String,

    required: [true, 'Name is required'],

    minlength: [3, 'Name must be at least 3
characters long']

  },

  email: {

    type: String,

    required: [true, 'Email is required'],

    unique: true,

    match: [/.+@.+\..+/, 'Please enter a valid
email address']
```

```
  },

  age: {

    type: Number,

    min: [18, 'Age must be at least 18']

  }

});
```

Explanation:

This adds constraints such as:

Name must be at least 3 characters long.

Email must match a specific pattern.

Age must be 18 or older.

> **Exercise:** Try saving a user with invalid data to see the validation errors.

Summary

In this chapter, we've covered:

The basics of MongoDB and how to set it up locally and on the cloud

How to use Mongoose to define models and schemas

CRUD operations with Mongoose

CHAPTER 8

BUILDING A RESTFUL API

... which covers building a RESTful API using Node.js and Express.

8.1 Introduction to RESTful APIs

APIs (Application Programming Interfaces) are a way for applications to communicate with each other. A RESTful API (Representational State Transfer API) is an architectural style for designing networked applications. RESTful APIs are stateless, making them simple to scale and manage. They use HTTP methods like GET, POST, PUT, and DELETE to interact with data.

Why RESTful APIs?

Flexibility: APIs are language-agnostic, allowing communication between different technologies.

Scalability: RESTful APIs are stateless, making them easy to scale horizontally.

Popularity: RESTful APIs are widely used and well-documented.

Example: RESTful APIs are used in web applications, mobile apps, and other services, like social media, where you fetch or update data.

8.2 Designing Your API

Before coding, it's essential to plan out the structure of the API. Key considerations include:

Resources: Each endpoint represents a "resource" (e.g., users, posts, orders).

HTTP Methods: The action performed on resources:

GET: Retrieve data

POST: Create new data

PUT: Update existing data

DELETE: Remove data

URL Structure: Use clear, meaningful URLs that represent resources (e.g., /api/users, /api/products/:id).

Responses: Design responses to include relevant data and status codes (200, 201, 404, etc.).

> **Exercise:** Draw an outline for an API that manages users and their tasks, specifying each endpoint and its HTTP method.

8.3 Setting Up the Project for a RESTful API

1. Initialize a New Project:

   mkdir my-restful-api

   cd my-restful-api

   npm init -y

2. Install Dependencies:

   npm install express mongoose dotenv

3. Project Structure: Organize files to keep the project manageable:

   my-restful-api/

   ├── config/

   │   └── database.js

   ├── models/

   │   └── User.js

```
├── routes/

│   └── users.js

├── controllers/

│   └── userController.js

├── .env

├── server.js

└── package.json
```

4. Environment Variables:

In .env, store sensitive information:

MONGO_URI=your_mongodb_connection string

PORT=3000

Tip: Use .env to separate sensitive data from your codebase, keeping your application secure.

8.4 Connecting to MongoDB

Use Mongoose to establish a connection to MongoDB.

In config/database.js:

const mongoose = require('mongoose');

const connectDB = async () => {

  try {

    await mongoose.connect(process.env.MONGO_URI, {

      useNewUrlParser: true,

      useUnifiedTopology: true

```
    type: String,

    required: true,

    unique: true

  },

  age: {

    type: Number,

    required: false

  }

});

const User = mongoose.model('User',
userSchema);

module.exports = User;
```

> **Exercise:** Add additional fields like password or role to the User schema to practice model creation.

8.6 Building RESTful Endpoints

Now, let's create routes and controllers to manage User resources. We'll focus on CRUD operations.

1. Setting Up Routes

    In routes/users.js:

    ```
    const express = require('express');

    const router = express.Router();

    const          userController          =
    require('../controllers/userController');

    router.post('/', userController.createUser);

    router.get('/', userController.getUsers);

    router.get('/:id',
    userController.getUserById);

    router.put('/:id',
    userController.updateUser);
    ```

```
router.delete('/:id',
userController.deleteUser);

module.exports = router;
```

In server.js, use the routes:

```
const            userRoutes         =
require('./routes/users');

app.use('/api/users', userRoutes);
```

2. Creating the Controller

The controller handles business logic, keeping routes clean.

In controllers/userController.js:

```
const User = require('../models/User');

// Create a new user

exports.createUser = async (req, res) => {

  try {
```

```
    const user = new User(req.body);

    await user.save();

    res.status(201).json(user);

  } catch (error) {

    res.status(400).json({              error:
error.message });

  }

};

// Get all users

exports.getUsers = async (req, res) => {

  try {

    const users = await User.find();

    res.json(users);

  } catch (error) {
```

```
    res.status(500).json({                error:
error.message }));

  }

};

// Get user by ID

exports.getUserById = async (req, res) => {

  try {

    const      user      =       await
User.findById(req.params.id);

    if  (!user)  return  res.status(404).json({
message: 'User not found' });

    res.json(user);

  } catch (error) {

    res.status(500).json({                error:
error.message }));

  }
```

```
};

// Update user by ID

exports.updateUser = async (req, res) => {

  try {

    const user = await
    User.findByIdAndUpdate(req.params.id,
    req.body, { new: true });

    if (!user) return res.status(404).json({
    message: 'User not found' });

    res.json(user);

  } catch (error) {

    res.status(400).json({ error:
    error.message });

  }

};

// Delete user by ID
```

```
exports.deleteUser = async (req, res) => {

try {

const user = await
User.findByIdAndDelete(req.params.id);

if (!user) return res.status(404).json({
message: 'User not found' });

res.json({ message: 'User deleted' });

} catch (error) {

res.status(500).json({ error:
error.message });

}

};
```

Exercise: Test each endpoint using a tool like Postman or Insomnia. Send requests to POST, GET, PUT, and DELETE users and observe the responses.

8.7 Testing and Debugging the API

Testing is essential for maintaining quality and reliability. Here's how to test the API:

1. Use Postman or Insomnia:

    Create requests for each endpoint (POST, GET, PUT, DELETE) with necessary data.

    Check response codes to ensure correctness (e.g., 201 for created, 200 for successful retrieval, 404 for not found).

2. Handle Errors Gracefully:

    Ensure that errors return appropriate status codes.

    Use try-catch blocks in controllers to handle unexpected issues.

3. Sample Test Flow:

    Create a new user, verify data in the response.

Retrieve the user by ID to confirm it was saved.

Update the user's information and confirm the response reflects changes.

Delete the user and ensure it's removed from the database.

Tip: Consider using automated testing tools like Jest or Mocha for more advanced testing setups in larger projects.

8.8 Best Practices for RESTful API Design

Following best practices can enhance the usability, security, and maintainability of your API.

Implement Pagination: When handling large datasets, implementing pagination reduces load times and makes your API more responsive. For example, instead of returning all users in a single response, split results by pages.

Example: /api/users?page=1&limit=10 to fetch 10 users per page.

Versioning: As your API grows, you may need to make changes without breaking existing clients. Use versioning in your URLs (e.g., /api/v1/users) to ensure backward compatibility.

Secure Sensitive Data: Avoid sending sensitive information like passwords or API keys in responses. If necessary, use encryption or hashing for any sensitive data stored or transmitted.

Rate Limiting: To protect your API from misuse and overuse, consider setting a rate limit to control the number of requests a client can make. Libraries like express-rate-limit in Node.js help manage this.

Use HTTP Headers: Leverage HTTP headers to provide metadata about the request and response. Common headers include Authorization for access tokens, Content-Type for specifying content format, and Cache-Control for caching policies.

Enable CORS (Cross-Origin Resource Sharing): If your API will be accessed by clients from different domains, configure CORS to allow cross-origin requests. This can be done in Express with the CORS middleware:

```
const cors = require('cors');

app.use(cors());
```

> **Exercise**: Implement basic rate limiting and CORS in your API to practice securing your endpoints.

8.9 Documenting Your API

API documentation helps developers understand how to use your endpoints, making integration easier for other teams and applications.

Using Swagger for Documentation

1. Install Swagger Tools:

    npm install swagger-jsdoc swagger-ui-express

2. Set Up Swagger Documentation by creating a swagger.js file to define the API schema:

    const swaggerJsDoc = require('swagger-jsdoc');

    const swaggerUi = require('swagger-ui-express');

    const swaggerOptions = {

```
swaggerDefinition: {

openapi: '3.0.0',

info: {

title: 'User API',

version: '1.0.0',

description: 'A simple Express API for
managing users'

},

servers: [

{

url: 'http://localhost:3000/api'

}

]

},

apis: ['./routes/*.js']
```

```
};

const          swaggerDocs          =
swaggerJsDoc(swaggerOptions);

module.exports = (app) => {

  app.use('/api-docs',          swaggerUi.serve,
swaggerUi.setup(swaggerDocs));

};
```

3. Annotate Your Routes with Swagger Comments:

In routes/users.js, add comments to generate documentation automatically:

```
/**

 * @swagger

 * /users:

 *   get:

 *     summary: Retrieve a list of users
```

```
 *     responses:

 *       200:

 *         description: A list of users

 *         content:

 *           application/json:

 *             schema:

 *               type: array

 *               items:

 *                                 $ref:
'#/components/schemas/User'

 */
```

```
router.get('/', userController.getUsers);
```

4. Enable Swagger in Your Server:

   Import and use the Swagger module in server.js:

```
const swagger = require('./swagger');

swagger(app);
```

5. Access the Documentation:

Start your server and visit http://localhost:3000/api-docs to see the auto-generated Swagger UI.

Tip: Good documentation includes example requests, responses, and any constraints on data formats.

8.10 Testing Your API with Postman

Postman is a popular tool for testing APIs. It allows you to send requests to each endpoint and view responses, making debugging easier.

Using Postman to Test CRUD Operations

1. Create a New Collection: Organize requests for your API in a collection.

2. Test Each Endpoint:

   POST /api/users: Create a user by sending JSON data.

   GET /api/users: Retrieve the list of users.

   GET /api/users/{id}: Retrieve a user by ID.

   PUT /api/users/{id}: Update a user by ID.

   DELETE /api/users/{id}: Delete a user by ID.

3. Check Status Codes and Data:

Verify that each request returns the expected status code (e.g., 201 for create, 200 for success, 404 for not found).

Validate that data in the response matches the structure and content you defined.

Exercise: Create a Postman collection with requests for each CRUD operation. Practice using Postman's environment variables to dynamically set request URLs and IDs.

8.11 Deployment Considerations for Your API

Once your API is ready, deploying it to a live server makes it accessible to clients. Here are some common deployment steps:

1. Choosing a Hosting Platform - Popular hosting platforms include:

   Heroku: Beginner-friendly, offers free tiers for small projects.

   DigitalOcean: Offers more control over your environment with virtual private servers.

   AWS, Google Cloud, and Microsoft Azure: Provide robust, scalable solutions for larger applications.

2. Preparing for Deployment

   Environment Variables: Use environment variables for configuration. Tools like dotenv help manage these variables locally, while hosting platforms allow setting them on the server.

Enable Production Logging: Configure logging for debugging and error tracking in production.

Handle Errors Gracefully: Ensure your API returns user-friendly error messages and status codes, even when unexpected errors occur.

3. Deploying to Heroku (Example)

- Install the Heroku CLI: Download and install the Heroku CLI from Heroku's website.

- Log in to Heroku: heroku login

- Create a Heroku Application:
  heroku create my-restful-api

4. Set Environment Variables - Add your MongoDB URI as a config variable:

heroku   config:set
MONGO_URI=your_mongodb_connection
_string

5. Deploy Your Code - Commit your code to Git:

git init

git add .

git commit -m "Initial commit"

Push to Heroku:

git push heroku master

Tip: Regularly monitor your deployed application's performance and logs, especially after updates or feature additions.

8.12 Securing Your API

APIs exposed to the internet must be secure to prevent unauthorized access. Here are key measures to protect your API:

Use Authentication and Authorization:

Implement token-based authentication (e.g., JWT) to verify users.

Use role-based access control (RBAC) to restrict access based on user roles (e.g., admin vs. regular user).

Data Validation and Sanitization:

Use libraries like express-validator to validate and sanitize inputs, preventing SQL injection and other attacks.

Encrypt Sensitive Data:

Use HTTPS to secure data in transit.

Avoid storing sensitive data in plaintext in the database.

Limit Data Exposure:

Only include necessary data in responses to avoid exposing sensitive information.

> **Exercise:** Try implementing basic JWT authentication on your API and configure permissions for different roles.

Summary

In this chapter, we've covered the essentials of building a RESTful API using Node.js, Express, and MongoDB. We went through:

Designing and structuring a REST API.

Setting up and connecting a MongoDB database using Mongoose.

Creating routes and controllers for CRUD operations.

Testing with Postman and ensuring responses are meaningful and standardized.

Documenting your API with Swagger for easy use by other developers.

Implementing best practices for deployment and security to make your API production-ready.

This concludes Chapter 8 on building RESTful APIs. This chapter should equipped you with skills and best practices for creating, testing, deploying, and securing your APIs.

With these skills, you are equipped to create and deploy reliable and secure APIs that can serve as backbones for web applications, mobile apps, and other services.

CHAPTER 9

AUTHENTICATION AND SESSION MANAGEMENT

... explore key techniques for implementing secure user authentication and managing sessions in your backend using Node.js and Express. You'll learn how to use JSON Web Tokens (JWTs) for stateless authentication, as well as other concepts necessary for securely handling user sessions. By the end of this chapter, you should be able to:

Understand the difference between authentication and authorization.

Set up JWT-based authentication in Node.js.

Create login and registration routes.

Secure routes with authentication middleware.

Implement basic session management techniques.

9.1 Understanding Authentication and Authorization

Before diving into code, it's essential to understand the key concepts that underpin secure applications.

Authentication: Verifying the identity of a user. For example, checking that a username and password match a registered user's credentials.

Authorization: Granting or denying access to specific resources based on a user's role or permissions. For instance, allowing only administrators to delete data.

In a RESTful API, we often implement stateless authentication, meaning each request from a client contains the necessary credentials (like a token) for verification. This approach is useful for APIs and scalable applications.

9.2 Using JSON Web Tokens (JWT) for Authentication

JSON Web Tokens (JWTs) are an industry-standard for securely transmitting information between a client and server. JWTs allow for stateless authentication, making them ideal for RESTful APIs.

Setting Up JWT in Node.js

1. Install JWT Package:

   npm install jsonwebtoken bcryptjs

Explanation:

jsonwebtoken provides the functionality for creating and verifying JWTs.

bcryptjs is a popular library for hashing passwords.

2. Configure Environment Variables:

Store a JWT_SECRET in a .env file to sign tokens:

JWT_SECRET=my_super_secret_key

Creating Tokens

A JWT has three parts: Header, Payload, and Signature. To generate a token, you encode user data (e.g., user ID) with a secret key.

Creating an Authentication Controller

In a new authController.js file:

```
const jwt = require('jsonwebtoken');

const bcrypt = require('bcryptjs');

const User = require('../models/User');
```

```
// Register a new user

exports.register = async (req, res) => {

  try {

    const { username, password } = req.body;

    const hashedPassword = await
bcrypt.hash(password, 10);

    const newUser = new User({ username,
password: hashedPassword });

    await newUser.save();

    res.status(201).json({ message: 'User
registered successfully' });

  } catch (error) {

    res.status(500).json({ error: 'Registration
failed' });

  }

};
```

```javascript
// Login a user and provide a token

exports.login = async (req, res) => {

  try {

    const { username, password } = req.body;

    const user = await User.findOne({ username
});

    if (!user || !(await bcrypt.compare(password,
user.password))) {

      return res.status(401).json({ error: 'Invalid
credentials' });

    }

    const token = jwt.sign({ id: user._id },
process.env.JWT_SECRET, { expiresIn: '1h' });

    res.json({ message: 'Login successful', token
});

  } catch (error) {
```

```
res.status(500).json({ error: 'Login failed' });

  }

};
```

Explanation: The register function hashes a new user's password and saves it, while the login function verifies the credentials and generates a JWT if they're correct.

Creating Secure Routes with JWT

1. Add Middleware to Verify JWT:

   Create a middleware function to protect routes by verifying JWT tokens.

   ```
   const jwt = require('jsonwebtoken');

   const authenticateToken = (req, res, next) => {
   ```

```
const                  token                =
req.header('Authorization')?.split(' ')[1];

if (!token) return res.status(403).json({
error: 'Access denied' });

jwt.verify(token,
process.env.JWT_SECRET, (err, user) => {

if (err) return res.status(403).json({
error: 'Invalid token' });

req.user = user;

next();

});

};

module.exports = authenticateToken;
```

2. Secure Routes Using Middleware:

To protect routes, apply the authenticateToken middleware:

```
const          authenticateToken      =
require('../middleware/authenticateToken')
;

router.get('/protected', authenticateToken,
(req, res) => {

  res.json({ message: 'This is a protected
route' });

});
```

9.3 Implementing Registration and Login Endpoints

Now that we have our JWT setup, let's build registration and login routes that allow users to sign up and log in.

1. Define Routes in authRoutes.js:

```
const express = require('express');

const          authController          =
require('../controllers/authController');
```

```
const router = express.Router();

router.post('/register',
authController.register);

router.post('/login', authController.login);

module.exports = router;
```

2. Add Routes to Your App:

In server.js, integrate the new routes:

```
const           authRoutes          =
require('./routes/authRoutes');

app.use('/auth', authRoutes);
```

> **Exercise:** Test the registration and login routes with Postman. Register a user, then log in with their credentials to obtain a token. Use the token to access a protected route.

9.4 Implementing Role-Based Access Control (RBAC)

With JWT-based authentication, you can also implement role-based access control (RBAC) to restrict access to specific endpoints.

1. Adding Roles to User Model:

   Update the User model to include a role field (e.g., admin, user).

   const mongoose = require('mongoose');

   const userSchema = new mongoose.Schema({

     username: String,

     password: String,

     role: { type: String, default: 'user' } // Default role is user

   });

```
module.exports = mongoose.model('User',
userSchema);
```

2. Creating Role-Based Middleware:

Define middleware to check if a user has a required role.

```
const authorizeRole = (role) => (req, res,
next) => {

  if (req.user.role !== role) {

    return     res.status(403).json({     error:
'Access denied' });

  }

  next();

};

module.exports = authorizeRole;
```

3. Protecting Admin Routes:

Apply role-based middleware to specific routes.

```
const          authorizeRole      =
require('../middleware/authorizeRole');

router.delete('/admin/delete-user',
authenticateToken, authorizeRole('admin'),
(req, res) => {

  // Admin-only logic here

});
```

9.5 Basic Session Management

In traditional web apps, sessions are used to keep track of authenticated users. Although JWT-based APIs don't need server-based sessions, session management can still be useful in cases like e-commerce carts or tracking activity.

Using express-session for Session Management

1. Install express-session:

   npm install express-session

2. Configure express-session in server.js:

   ```
   const session = require('express-session');

   app.use(session({

     secret: process.env.SESSION_SECRET,

     resave: false,

     saveUninitialized: true,

     cookie: { secure: false } // Set to true in production for HTTPS

   }));
   ```

3. Using Sessions in Routes:

```
app.get('/set-session', (req, res) => {

  req.session.userId = '12345';

  res.send('Session set');

});

app.get('/get-session', (req, res) => {

  res.send(`User ID in session:
${req.session.userId}`);

});
```

Note: Use sessions only when necessary, as they increase server load.

Summary

In Chapter 9, we covered how to implement secure authentication and manage user sessions. Key points include:

Understanding the difference between authentication and authorization.

Setting up JWT-based authentication for a stateless API.

Creating registration and login endpoints.

Implementing role-based access control (RBAC) for restricted routes.

Configuring basic session management when necessary.

With these skills, your API can securely handle user authentication, allowing you to develop more complex applications with confidence.

CHAPTER 10

DATA VALIDATION AND ERROR HANDLING

... covers the essential skills of data validation and error handling to ensure the robustness and reliability of your Node.js backend. You'll learn how to validate incoming data to protect against invalid or malicious input, and how to manage errors effectively to make debugging and user feedback more manageable. By the end of this chapter, you will be able to:

Implement data validation using popular libraries.

Set up custom validation rules.

Manage errors and send meaningful error messages.

Structure error handling with middleware.

10.1 Importance of Data Validation

Data validation ensures that any data your application processes, especially from users or third-party sources, meets the expected format and constraints. By validating data, you:

Prevent incorrect or harmful data from entering your system.

Improve user experience by providing meaningful feedback on errors.

Avoid security risks such as injection attacks.

10.2 Setting Up Data Validation with Joi

Joi is a widely-used validation library that makes it easy to define and apply data validation rules.

Installing Joi

First, install Joi in your project:

    npm install joi

Creating a Validation Schema

In a Node.js app, we typically define a validation schema for each entity, such as User, Product, or Post. Let's create a simple schema for a User model.

In a new file called validation.js, add the following:

```
const Joi = require('joi');

const userSchema = Joi.object({

  username: Joi.string().min(3).max(30).required(),

  email: Joi.string().email().required(),

  password: Joi.string().min(6).required(),

});

module.exports = { userSchema };
```

Here's what the schema specifies:

username: Must be a string between 3 and 30 characters.

email: Must be a valid email format.

password: Must be at least 6 characters.

Applying Validation in Routes

To apply this validation in your routes, use Joi to validate the request body before proceeding with any further logic.

In your registration route (e.g., in authController.js):

```
const { userSchema } = require('../validation');

exports.register = async (req, res) => {

  const { error } = userSchema.validate(req.body);
```

```
    if (error) return res.status(400).json({
    error: error.details[0].message });

    // Proceed with registration logic

};
```

Explanation: Here, we validate req.body against userSchema. If validation fails, we return a 400 status with an error message; otherwise, we proceed.

10.3 Custom Validation Rules

Sometimes, you may need custom validation rules. Joi allows you to create specific rules to handle these cases.

For instance, you could add a rule to prevent usernames containing certain words:

```
const userSchema = Joi.object({

  username: Joi.string()

    .min(3)

    .max(30)

    .regex(/^(?!.*(admin|root)).*$/,
'restricted words')

    .required(),

  email: Joi.string().email().required(),

  password: Joi.string().min(6).required(),

});
```

> **Note:** In this example, we added a regular expression rule to restrict username from containing "admin" or "root." This customization helps prevent unwanted names that could be confusing or misleading for users.

10.4 Centralized Error Handling

Node.js applications can have a variety of error sources, from user input to system-level issues. A centralized error-handling approach makes it easier to manage these errors consistently.

Creating an Error Handling Middleware

Express allows you to define error-handling middleware, which lets you intercept and process errors in a single place.

In a new file called errorMiddleware.js, create an error handler:

// errorMiddleware.js

const errorHandler = (err, req, res, next) => {

  console.error(err.stack);   // Log the stack trace for debugging

  res.status(500).json({ error: 'An unexpected error occurred!' });

```
};
```

```
module.exports = errorHandler;
```

Adding Error Middleware to Your App

Include the error-handling middleware in your main server file (server.js), placing it at the end of all other routes and middleware:

```
const           errorHandler           =
require('./middleware/errorMiddleware');
```

```
// Other routes and middleware
```

```
app.use(errorHandler);
```

> **Note:** This will catch any errors that are thrown in your routes and send a generic message back to the client.

10.5 Handling Validation Errors

To provide more specific error messages for validation errors, you can modify the error middleware to check if the error is from Joi validation.

Update errorMiddleware.js as follows:

```
const errorHandler = (err, req, res, next) => {

  if (err.isJoi) {

    return res.status(400).json({ error: err.details[0].message });

  }

  console.error(err.stack);

  res.status(500).json({ error: 'An unexpected error occurred!' });

};

module.exports = errorHandler;
```

Explanation: Here, if the error is a Joi validation error, we return a 400 status with the specific message from Joi, providing clearer feedback to the user.

10.6 Managing Common Errors in Node.js Applications

Besides validation errors, there are several types of common errors you should anticipate and handle:

1. Database Errors:

   If your app can't connect to the database, log the error, and provide a helpful message for further diagnosis.

2. 404 Errors (Not Found):

   If a requested route or resource is not found, return a 404 status with a clear message.

   app.use((req, res) => {

     res.status(404).json({ error: 'Route not found' });

   });

3. Authentication and Authorization Errors:

   Return 401 Unauthorized for authentication failures.

   Return 403 Forbidden for permission issues.

4. Timeouts:

If a request takes too long, set a timeout to avoid the application hanging indefinitely.

```
app.use((req, res, next) => {

  res.setTimeout(5000, () => {

    return res.status(503).json({ error: 'Request timed out' });

  });

  next();

});
```

10.7 Testing and Debugging Errors

A systematic approach to testing and debugging is essential for error handling. Here are a few methods:

1. Testing with Postman:

   Use Postman to send requests to your API endpoints, testing for various scenarios like missing fields, incorrect data, and unauthorized access.

2. Console Logging:

   Use console.log and console.error to log errors and inspect data. Logging can help identify what went wrong during request processing.

3. Debugging with Node Inspector:

Use Node's built-in inspector by running your app with the inspect flag:

node inspect server.js

This enables breakpoints and step-by-step debugging, which is helpful in isolating issues in the code.

4. Automated Testing:

Write tests for your validation and error-handling logic. Frameworks like Jest and Mocha allow you to test if your validation rules work as expected and if your middleware correctly handles errors.

Summary

In Chapter 10, you learned the essentials of data validation and error handling, both critical for building reliable, user-friendly applications. Key takeaways include:

Setting up and using Joi for input validation.

Applying custom validation rules to suit your app's requirements.

Implementing centralized error-handling middleware in Express.

Managing common types of errors such as validation, database, and authentication errors.

Testing and debugging to improve the robustness of error handling.

With these tools, you can ensure that your backend handles data consistently and recovers gracefully from errors, providing a more stable and professional experience for users.

CHAPTER 11

DEPLOYING YOUR NODEJS APPLICATION

In this final chapter, we'll guide you through deploying your Node.js application to production. Deploying means hosting your application on a server so it's accessible over the internet, allowing real users to interact with it. By the end of this chapter, you will know:

How to prepare your app for production.
The basics of environment variables for managing configurations.
Step-by-step deployment on a popular platform (Heroku).
Basic maintenance tips for a production environment.

11.1 Preparing for Deployment

Before deploying, it's important to optimize and prepare your app for a production environment. Let's look at a few critical steps.

Setting Environment Variables with dotenv

Environment variables are essential for securely managing sensitive data like API keys and configuration values. In this section, we'll install and configure the dotenv package to simplify managing these variables.

1. Installing dotenv: Open your terminal in your project folder and run the following command to install dotenv:

   npm install dotenv

Explanation: npm install dotenv tells Node.js to download and add dotenv to your project. This package allows you to store configuration

values in a separate .env file instead of hardcoding them in your application code.

2. Creating a .env File: In the root of your project directory, create a new file named .env.

Tip: Ensure this file is in the same directory as your server.js or main application file.

3. Adding Configuration Variables to .env: Open the .env file and add any sensitive data or configuration values, like your app's port or database connection string. Here's an example:

PORT=3000

DB_URI=your_database_url

SECRET_KEY=your_secret_key

4. Configuring dotenv in Your Application: Open your main application file (server.js) and add the following line at the very top:

```
require('dotenv').config();
```

Explanation: This line loads the variables from .env into process.env, making them accessible throughout your app. Now, you can reference any environment variable by using process.env.VARIABLE_NAME.

5. Accessing Environment Variables in Code: For example, to use the port variable in your app, modify your server's listen method as follows:

```
const port = process.env.PORT || 3000;

app.listen(port, () => {
```

```
    console.log(`Server    running    on    port
${port}`);

});
```

6. Protecting Your .env File: Add .env to your .gitignore file to prevent this sensitive data from being uploaded to version control (e.g., GitHub). This ensures your secrets remain private.

   # Add this line to your .gitignore file

   .env

11.2 Selecting a Deployment Platform

There are several popular platforms for deploying Node.js applications, including Heroku, DigitalOcean, and AWS. For simplicity, we'll demonstrate deploying to

Heroku, which is beginner-friendly and provides free hosting for small projects.

11.3 Deploying on Heroku

Setting Up Heroku CLI:

1. Install Heroku CLI: Download and install the Heroku CLI from Heroku's website.

2. Log in to Heroku: After installation, open your terminal and log in:

   heroku login

Preparing Your Project for Heroku:

1. Specify a Start Script: In your package.json file, set the start script to run your server. Heroku will look for this script when launching the app.

```
"scripts": {

  "start": "node server.js"

}
```

2. Set Your App Port: In your server.js file, use process.env.PORT to allow Heroku to set the port dynamically.

```
const port = process.env.PORT || 3000;

app.listen(port, () => {

  console.log(`Server running on port ${port}`);

});
```

Deploying Your Application:

1. Initialize Git: Ensure your project is under version control with Git.

```
git init

git add .

git commit -m "Initial commit"
```

2. Create a Heroku App: In the terminal, create a new app on Heroku.

   heroku create your-app-name

3. Deploy Your Code: Push your code to Heroku's Git repository.

   git push heroku master

4. Set Up Environment Variables: If your app requires environment variables (e.g., DB_URI or SECRET_KEY), you need to set these in Heroku.

   heroku   config:set
   DB_URI=your_database_url
   SECRET_KEY=your_secret_key

5. Open Your App: Once deployed, open your app to see it live:

   heroku open

Tip: Heroku provides basic logs that can help you debug if there are any deployment issues. You can view them with:

heroku logs --tail

11.4 Monitoring and Maintenance

After deployment, monitoring and maintaining your application becomes essential to ensure it runs smoothly and scales as needed.

Logging and Error Monitoring:

1. Basic Logging: Use console.log for basic logging during development. In production, a logging tool like Winston or Morgan can help capture and organize logs.

2. Error Monitoring Services: Services like Sentry or LogRocket provide more advanced error monitoring and allow you to track issues over time.

Scaling and Managing Resources:

As your app grows, you may need more resources. Heroku allows you to scale by increasing the number of dynos (containers) running your app. You can do this through the Heroku dashboard or the CLI:

heroku ps:scale web=1 # Increase dyno count if needed

Note: Free plans on Heroku may "sleep" if inactive for a certain period. Upgrading to a paid plan avoids this and provides more consistent performance.

11.5 Testing and Debugging in Production

Testing your application in a production environment helps identify any issues that may not appear in development.

1. Use Postman for Live Testing: Send requests to your deployed endpoints to ensure everything works as expected.

2. Health Checks: Implement basic health-check routes to test if the app is running. For example:

```
app.get('/health', (req, res) => {

  res.send('Server is up and running!');

});
```

3. Error Handling: Make sure your error-handling middleware provides meaningful messages and does not expose sensitive data.

Summary

In Chapter 11, you learned the essentials of deploying your Node.js application, from preparing your code to hosting it on Heroku. Key takeaways include:

Setting environment variables to securely manage configurations.

Deploying on Heroku with step-by-step guidance, including initializing Git, creating a Heroku app, and pushing your code.

Monitoring your application's health and managing errors in production.

Scaling resources on Heroku as your application grows.

This chapter completes your journey in building and deploying a Node.js backend application. You now have a full understanding of how to develop, secure, and deploy your app,

bringing it from a local development environment to a live production platform.

www.ingramcontent.com/pod-product-compliance
Lightning Source LLC
LaVergne TN
LVHW051639050326
832903LV00022B/815